FROM THE DAFTER
EDGES
OF ABSURDITY

**All proceeds from this book go to
Macmillan Cancer Relief**

Charity number: 261017

FROM THE DAFTER

EDGES

OF ABSURDITY

by
John McMillan

Foreword by William McIlvanney

Published by John McMillan
1998

Published by John McMillan
Invergordon, Ross-shire
1998

ISBN: 0 9533116 0 0

Printed by : Gospel Truth Press, Invergordon.

This Book is Dedicated to

The Macmillan Nurses

FOREWORD

Many years ago, when the world was young, I taught English in the same Ayrshire school where John McMillan taught mathematics. This was BPC (Before Political Correctness), when taking the merciless mickey out of friends was still a national pastime in Scotland and happy insult was still legal tender.

In those primitive times strange behaviour flourished. I remember with affection the science teacher who had trouble controlling classes. His solution was beautifully simple and a fine example of lateral thinking (rather similar to Arthur Scott's cunning in *Take Up The Slack*). Instead of doing anything as ordinary as bringing the class to order, he rigged up a tannoy system in his small lab. By this simple method, he could broadcast his lesson to the general mêlée and anybody who was odd enough to want to work could at least hear what he was saying. I always thought there was something slightly heroic about that, a kind of Radio Cuba subversiveness.

The science teacher was not alone in his eccentricity. Among all the weird contortions into which human nature gets itself without even noticing how bizarre it is being, I have a memory of John McMillan's quizzical face looking on with some bemusement. I can still see that face lurking behind these verses.

It's good to know that John McMillan's eye for the absurd has remained undimmed over all these years and still looks on the oddities of the world with a kind amazement. From the *Power of Prayer* to the orange juice strike, Acky's bullfight and Dennis Scott's *Special Offer*, I enjoyed reading these unpretentious poems. Although they are about people in a particular locality, they have features that should be recognisable to us all. If we are honest, we may see some of those features in the mirror.

Enjoyable in themselves, these verses are also a good way of reminding us of some of our own more ludicrous doings - like putting our egos on a diet. I hope John McMillan keeps watching and reporting back from some of the dafter edges of absurdity.

William McIlvanney
8 April 1998

Introduction

I'm nae a poet, in a sense
But just a rhymer like by chance - Robert Burns

Since making a crude attempt at chronicling, in verse, events in the lives of the people of Ardross at the Burns Supper in the village hall in 1985 I have had no peace. For ever since people have been whispering in my ear bits of gossip about their neighbours, prefixed by: "Here's wan for the next Burns Supper". Life in a rural community is never dull.

This book is a collection of short stories in verse recording the antics of some of the 'characters' of that part of Easter Ross which includes Alness, Ardross, Invergordon, Barbaraville and Delny. Most of the stories are based on truth, though the discerning reader may detect a hint of poetic licence.

The characters in these pages are likely to be recognised in any rural community. There are men who have yet to unshackle themselves from the yolk of chauvinism; political correctness has yet to infiltrate their personal protocol. Their mode of expression is often colourful, and best appreciated in the hearing, rather than in the harsh, impersonal appearance of the words in print!

My neighbour, farmer Acky Davidson, is a man whose enthusiastic and eloquent use of the Anglo Saxon expletive is comically inoffensive and has inspired so many of the stories in this book. Long may he flourish!

The man who has buried so much of the district's garbage, Alistair Ross, The Rooster, has to expect a bit of a roasting with such a nickname. Like Tam o Shanter and Souter Johnny, The Rooster and his erstwhile drinking partner, skilled shepherd Bobby Low, have ensured a healthy balance in the excise coffers and inspired a series of comic tales about their exploits, often recounted with glee by skilled story-tellers George and Urquhart Morrison and retired grieve Dennis Scott.

These are some of the characters who frequent the Old Dutch Barn, a couthy howf in a converted steading owned by Dutchman Eddy Robberts and his family. Eddy has defied the rules of economics by running a successful holiday chalet business with some farming on the side for the past twenty years here. He could well set up as a consultant in obtaining grants.

I must also express my appreciation of the tolerance and good nature of the ladies of Ardross Women's Rural Institute, whose friendship has been valued for so many years and whose mischievous sense of fun has fuelled my pen so often. And they still ask for more.

I am indebted to many people for their help and encouragement in producing this volume; to the sponsors and those who have donated photographs; Mairi Kemp for her help in editing; Julie Simmons who spent many hours working on illustrations and cover design, for steering the publication through its production and for arranging its launch while I was abroad. It would never have happened without her enthusiastic nagging but och, it kept her off the street.

Every penny raised by the sale of this book will support the excellent work done by the Macmillan Nurses in providing the best possible care at home for cancer patients and their families in the Highlands.

John McMillan
April 1998.

Contents

A RIPPING YARN

After mating his ferrets George Morrison asked his wife Dorothy to bring a saucer of milk to the buck to restore its energy. The buck had plenty to spare however and expressed a preference for Dorothy's charms, providing an interesting insight into everyday Highland life for some visitors from the south.

George Morrison's ferret's mighty handy;
At catching rabbits it's a dandy,
But, one day, it got unco randy
And ran berserk,
Comsumed wi' lust for houghmagandie,
Up Dorothy's skirt!

Though Dorothy's a douce wee woman,
The horny devil fair had her screamin'
And George cried oot, " Haud still, I'm comin'."
For this was drastic.
The ferret's claws were fairly strummin'
On her elastic!

As Dorothy's roars rang oot like thunder,
George didnae stand and gaze in wonder.
He thrust his heid right up and under,
For close inspection;
To where the ferret tore asunder,
Dot's sole protection.

Visitors next door heard her cries,
Rushed oot wi' panic in their eyes
And stood, in stupified surprise,
At this uproar.
As the ferret groped at Dorothy's thighs,
Her undies tore!

Poor Dorothy fainted in a swoon,
But Geordie's a phlegmatic loon
And when he'd got the ferret doon
And put away,
He nodded to those gathered roon,
"Aye, Aye, fine day".

THE ACK ACK GUN

(In memory of the day Ardross survived an air raid!)

It was 1988 - 27 November,
When Ardross got into the news
For an RAF Jaguar aircraft
Dropped its bombs on the Achnacloich coos!

By good fortune, the innocent bovines
Survived and not one was hurt;
But the bombs dug a hole in their pasture
And threw up a big heap o' dirt.

Poor Anthony Walker was toilin'
In the field at mending a drain,
But he never expected the heavens
To deluge him wi' that kind o' rain.

The effect on his bowels was dramatic!
And it lasted for two or three weeks;
For when Anthony saw the bombs dropping
He could've done wi' a drain in his breeks!

Aye, these screamin' jet planes are a problem
When they're flying so near to the ground;
They'll combine a field in a second,
And they make such a helluva sound.

Davie Fraser was buzzed at the balin',
One Tuesday night just after eight;
The pilot flung doon a wee letter,
"Would you please leave open the gate?"

George MacKay was a handsome young fermer
Wi' a guid crop o' ginger red hair,
But now, if you look at poor Geordie,
His locks are increasingly rare.

He'll tell you himsel', at the clippin',
One fine summer day he was oot,
When a low flying plane nearly topped him;
Since then he's been bald as a coot!

The bairns at the school get excited
By these menaces up in the air,
And every time one thunders over,
The infant's class aye wets the flair!

The folk in Ardross wrote a letter
To protest at the threat from the sky;
But the MOD just wouldnae listen,
So Ardross then declared UDI.

An election was held for Prime Minister;
Roland Mardon's the man that they got,
For wi' proportional representation
The Mardons had maist o' the vote!

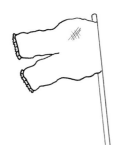

Roland set about raising an army
And conscripted every fit man,
To defend the freedom of Ardross;
(Fraser picked all four up in his van!)

But the first to respond to the muster
To tackle the threat from the sky,
Became known as the First Battalion
O' the Ardross W.R.I.

In their hand-knitted wool balaclavas
They prepared themselves for the wars,
And marched wi' their battle standard -
A pair o' Mrs Allison's drawers!

Roddy Coates cottoned on quite quickly
That an army requires a NAAFI,
And he set about puttin' a sign up,
O'er the door o' Pauline's wee cafe.

And just as they did in the last war,
When the Home Guard was then called upon,
Dad's Army, up here in Ardross,
Was Davie, George and Willie John.

(These geriatric fusiliers
Were armed for their adventures
Wi' walkin' sticks, and clippin' shears,
And Moira Shearer's dentures.)

Ritchie Martin went roon' wi' his bagpipes
To rally the Strathrusdale loons;
When they marched in style past the castle,
Eddie Scott joined in wi' his spoons.

Then Roland addressed all his forces:
"Now, look here chaps, it's plain commonsense,
If we're to emerge victorious,
We need to have some *air* defence".

Acky Davidson then interrupted:
"Nae problem! This f-frightful war's won,
(or words to that effect!)
I've had an idea for a weapon",
And they called it Ack's Ack Ack Gun.

"There's a stockpile o' good ammunition
In a field doon at Lower Kincraig;
Three hundred tons o' prime sewage,
And a helluva stink it has made!

"Wi' a high pressure pump and a hosepipe
Attached to a twenty ton tank,
We'll spray up a jet o' the slurry
And the atmosphere then will be rank".

When the first plane flew into the mist screen,
That Acky sprayed up wi' his hose,
The pilot smelled something offensive,
And started to wrinkle his nose.

"Ohhhh! Sierra Hotel India Tango,"
He cried doon the plane's intercom:
"They've found the ultimate deterrent,
It's worse than the hydrogen bomb!"

Then he turned back to Lossiemouth Air Base;
But, poor soul, it wasnae his day,
For the boys that man the control tower,
Had smelled him fae ten miles away!

"Keep away! Ye smell like a midden!
Ye'll hae to ditch oot in the sea
And steep yersel' two or three hours
Afore ye come hame for your tea!"

So, the planes gave Ardross a wide berth
Because o' the smell that was there,
And the odour zoomed up to the heavens,
Through yon hole in the Earth's ozone layer.

But.... a Russian sputnik was spyin'
As it silently cruised out in space,
By a chance in a million, its orbit
Took it right o'er Acky's place!

When the cosmonauts sniffed the foul odour,
They cried to their man, Gorbachev,
"Forget Reagan and Bush and their Star Wars,
Get Acky to turn that thing off!"

So peace here on Earth was established,
As well as up there in the skies,
And Acky was then nominated
To pick up the Nobel Peace Prize!

So, there's a lesson for fermers and gairdeners;
Don't forget, if it's problems ye face,
Just follow Acky's example
And spread heaps o' dung a' o'er the place.

EPISTLE TO AULD SCOTT

In 'This is Your Life' style , Dennis Scott was presented with a framed copy of these verses at a dinner he organised as a surprise for his family on his retirement. However, the surprise was on him when a man with a red book appeared!

Dear Scotty,
Is it really true or do my eyes deceive
That underwriting this whole feast is Dennis Scott the Grieve?
I hope, auld freen', ye'll think nae ill should I intrude your party,
Tae wish ye happy birthday - Boy, ye're lookin' hale and hearty!

Ye've reached a major milestone now, I hear ye're sixty five,
And fit for dancing jigs and reels, and whiles ye'll even Jive!
So to mark this anniversary, just sit there on your erse,
For the Muse just took a haud o' me, and listen to this verse

In a but an' ben near Forres in 1929,
Ye came screamin' tae the world and ye're bowels worked just fine.
Ye soon kent what a voice was for, for a' ye were sae wee,
Ye didnae need a clock tae tell ye it was time for tea!

Fate decreed that ye would leave the school, (though aye a lad o' pairts),
And had ye yokit tae the plough, and grapin' dung, and drivin' cairts.
Ye had an eye for breedin' stock, if ye follow what I mean,
For ye surely picked a winner when ye bid for Bonnie Jean.

Ye were just a bothy lad when ye went oot wan nicht tae dance,
But the instant that your eyes met hers, she had ye in a trance.
O'er forty years have passed since then and still she has ye fettered,
Fair play, ye're no' complainin', for ye ken she can't be bettered!

When it came to procreation ye've proved a worthy sire,
Ye only had wan hobby, and there's nae sign that ye'll tire!
A daughter and four sons owe their existence all to you,
But you're the first to say that maybe Jean deserves some credit too!

They've followed father's footsteps in the reproductive game
They bring their broods to you - and eat ye oot o' hoose and hame!
You're blessed wi' 13 gran' weans and they're aged from one to twenty,
The apple o' your eye - but 13 Christmas presents's plenty!

A crofter's life has aye been hard, and luxuries are few,
TV was quite auld-fashioned before it came to you.
But it used up electricity and the cash was hard to raise,
So the weans were strictly rationed to one programme - Songs of Praise!

One Christmas - ye were bidin' at a place doon near Kingussie -
It was proposed a Christmas tree would fairly brighten up the hoosie.
A tiny spruce was cut and placed upon the windae sill,
And then ye decorated it, wi' classic crofter skill.

Some cotton wool and tinsel served to imitate the snaw;
A coloured sweetie paper roon' one light bulb, that was a'
Ye could afford for decoration: an auld car battery gave the power
For the light bulb, and the job was neatly done in half an hour!

The family always got a holiday - ye were an enterprisin' man -
Ye packed up wife and weans and borrowed someone else's van.
The world was then your oyster, and to exotic parts you'd trail,
Jean enjoyed a change o' view - while peelin' tatties o'er a pail!

Your mind was aye alert when you were muckin' oot the byre.
One day, when Jean was drying a' the weans' claes by the fire,
A spark louped oot and burnt a hole in Charlie's romper suit,
But in an instant your keen mind had worked a nice wee fiddle oot!

You dashed quickly to the fireside, for you saw the need to hurry,
"That's whit we pay insurance for, so Jean, my dear, don't worry.
We'll soon get a' oor money back", and ye grabbed a glowing coal,
And in every stitch o' claes ye left a nice big blackened hole!

When it comes to economics, ye're in a class a' by yoursel'
The taxman failed to catch ye, and the bank's lost oot as well.
The British Telecom accountants can never match your skill,
Ye only make reverse-charge phone calls, so ye never get a bill!

But wan time ye were caught oot,when Jean gave oot a wail,
"I need a three-piece suite", and so ye went off to the sale.
Ye thocht ye'd saved a packet when ye bocht a nice new suite,
But ye were blinded by the discount and forgot to try the seat.

When the new suite was delivered and set up in the room,
Ye fidgeted and hummed and hawed, and then began to fume.
"This damned chair's no' sae comfy - my bum's too near the flair!"
So ye stormed oot tae the yard to resurrect your ain auld chair.

Again it occupied its rightful place beside the fire,
And once your bum was in it, ye began to lose your ire.
Now, when life is full of hardship and you're laden down wi' care
You ease away your worries, dozing in your favourite chair!

Ye've oiled the wheels o' commerce for the laird o' Balintraid,
And worked your ain wee croftie, aye, ye've been a busy lad,
Wi' your cattle, neeps and tatties; and everybody thinks,
That the keystone o' their diet is a plate o' Scott's Kerr's Pinks.

Ye've gained fame for couthy stories at the ceilidhs o'er the years;
Reputations are destroyed if secrets get to Scotty's ears!
That matchless sense o' humour is superlative, I think
That once I saw ye laugh so much, ye nearly bocht a drink!

Weel Scotty, now the time has come to free ye fae dissection,
In superannuated life you'll find time for inspection,
Of this humble poet's tribute to yourself and Jean your wife,
Thanks to your family, ye've been framed, so Dennis Scott,

This is Your Life.

BACK TO BASICS

At the Tory Party conference in 1993,
John Major coined a phrase the papers seized upon wi' glee.
Back to Basics was the slogan to rally round the party,
It was apt enough, for ministers' reputations were gey clarty!
There's plenty Holy Willies, and ye'll find the Unco Guid
Are not only in the kirks, there's plenty creepin' oot the wood.
There's hordes o' them pontificating, always hale and hearty,
And some are cabinet ministers in John Major's Tory Party!
The PM's in a pickle, he just canny shut their gobs,
He'll soon be lookin' in the papers at the adverts for the jobs!
Nae doubt he'll need to dae a bit o' drastic weedin' oot
Or his cabinet will send the Tory Party doon the shute.
Transport minister Steven Norris has been having it away,
But he's walked oot on his wife - och well, that makes it all OK.
Then there's whit's-his-name in Paris, in the papers it was said
There was only wan spare room and he'd to share a double bed.
There's anither yin ca'd Waller who's been on the ran dan dan,
David Ashby's left his wife for he's a prefers it wi' a man.
There's yon yin wi' the queer like name, they call him Yo Ho Ho,
Who's boldly gone where no man ever dared before to go.
A man's a man for a' that, and he has to pay the price,
But alas, it's no the first time, for he said he's done it twice!
Miss Jan Fitzallan Howard, I just canny understan',
Takin' on the Earl o' Caithness fur tae be her fancy man.
Wi' the tragic circumstances that came oot o' that affair,
His career is on the rocks - just like yon tanker ca'd the Braer.
Three million unemployed were thinking this is hard to thole,
When Caithness joined the queue, doon at the b'roo, to get his dole!
There's Mellor wi' his fitba gear: wasn't yon a proper farce?
He kept a model ca'd Angelica, just to boot him up the arse.
But then Angelica blew the whistle and the tabloids had their say,
And the Minister for Sport was aff the park for dirty play!

Still they're preachin' family values, "Back to Basics" is their motto,
While they fornicate away - and if they're no' they're aye half-blotto!
Single mothers are condemned by those who dwell in fleshly lust,
And they'll tell us at election time, they're guys that we can trust.
And they've the nerve to tell the nation that the weans there at the school,
Should play safe and use a condom and a contraceptive pill!
Mrs Bobbitt has the answer - and the politicians' wives
Should cut off the honourable members, in their beds wi' long sharp knives!
Then the cabinet would look a proper bunch of silly - billies
In the House of Commons lavy when they couldnae find their willies!

NEVER DRINK AND DRIVE

Now here's a tale, like Tam O' Shanter;
As Bobby Low, ae nicht did canter;
And ended up e'en mair perplexed,
Than Ernie Robberts is oversexed!

Poor Bobby's had a gey sair hip,
It fairly has been gie'n him gyp.
It was that bad he could scarcely walk,
So he had to go and see the doc.

"Just drap yer troosers o'er there",
Said the doctor, and began to stare,
At Bobby's problematic rump,
Fair play, his hip had got'n a hump.
Side-on, Bob looked like a camel,
Nae wonder it was sic a trammel.
The doctor's face took on a frown,
"The arthritis has fairly gone to town.
Ye'll no' go far in sic a state,
I'm afraid we'll have to operate.
A plastic hip will do the trick".
The thocht o' that made poor Bob sick,
And off he went wi' trembling lips,
To calm doon wi' a couple o' nips.

The operation went really well,
But hospital for Bob was hell.
Just lying there, a helpless cripple,
He dreamed about his favourite tipple.
As bottles swam before his eyes,
He thocht he was in paradise.
It wasnae Beaujolais fae France,
But whisky bottles in a dance!
They circled round him on the floor,
Laphroig, Glenmorangie and Dalmore;
But stayed beyond his frantic grip,
And left him thirstin' for a nip.
They reeled, they set, they crossed, they cleekit ,
Till Bobby woke up, swat and reekit,
And cried, "Dear God, this isnae fair!"
Each night he had the same nightmare.

When Bob got oot, he'd one desire -
To taste the amber nectar's fire,
And Bobby, now a desperate man,
Hirpled oot to his wee van.
His destination was the pub;
But ah, dear frien's, now here's the rub,
There's surely no' a man alive,
But kens ye shouldnae drink and drive.
But Bobby, filled wi' Famous Grouse,
Tried to drive back to the house.

He drove wi' style and flair and verve,
But then, the road began to swerve;
Bob drove straight on like ane bewitched
And couped the van right in the ditch!
The van got bent as it went o'er,
Nae wey could Bob get oot the door.
Undaunted, Bob without a care,
Just went to sleep while lying there.
But another motorist came along,
And saw that something had gone wrong.
With Bob, unconscious, lying inside,
Fair play, he thought the chiel had died!
The polis, fire brigade, ambulance too,
Were a' ca'd oot 'cause Bob was fu'!
He'll pay a hefty price for erring,
For Bob was pickled, like a herring.
Apart fae that, he was alright,
So they dumped him in the cells that night.

But wait now, that is not the end,
For next day Bobby phoned a friend.
"Could ye come and take me home?" said Bob.
"Nae bother. That's a simple job.
Which police station are ye at?"
Bob couldnae even answer that!
To let his friend perform the task,
"Is this Tain or Alness?" he had to ask.

Now wha this tale o' truth shall read,
Ilk man and mither's son tak' head,
Whene'er to drink you are inclined,
Just keep Bobby Low in mind;
And if ye want to stay alive,
Remember - never drink and drive!

CAVEAT

The best laid schemes o' mice and men gang aft agley : R Burns
Presented to Ian Goldsack MA, Depute Rector of Invergordon Academy
on his retirement.

One day, I went to Inverness,
And left my office in a mess;
Computer switched on, at its station,
Awaiting further information.
The green light on the printer too,
Showed it ready for its cue,
To chatter into action when
The laptop gave the appropriate sign.

No' much there that could go wrong?
Then Ian Goldsack came along.
For Ian then had just caught sight,
O' (through the door) that wee green light.
Computers left on bother Liz,
So, to stop her getting in a tizz,
Ian, (aye a considerate mannie),
Caring about Liz the Janny,
Thought he'd better shut it down,
And boy, he really went to town!

He strode across towards the table
But failed to see a trailing cable.
Now, maybe it was just a whim,
But boy, that cable sure saw him!
And Ian got an awfu' fleg,
When it wrapped itsel' right roon' his leg.
The mair he tried t' undo the fankle,
The tighter it gripped him roon' the ankle.
In panic, he let oot a roar,
And, just then, Liz came through the door.

Now here my muse her wing maun cour,
Sic flights are far beyond her pow'r,
To sing how Ian lap and flang,
A supple lad he was, and strang.
And how Liz stood like yin bewitched,
And thocht her very een enriched.

The laptop loupit in the air,
And crashed like thunder on the flair,
The printer, not to be outdone,
Decided it would join the fun
Wi' a back flip and a somersault,
(Performed without a single fault)
It smoored itsel' wi' fine black toner
And never worked again - nae won'er!

Now, Liz just stood richt sair astonished,
But wait now, Ian wasnae finished,
It takes a lot to make Ian curse,
Fair play, things went fae bad to worse!

He vainly tried to free himsel',
And muttered, "Damn!" and "Bloody Hell!"
Till first ae caper, syne anither',
Ian tint his reason a' t'gither,
And, in a fit o' sheer delirium,
Lost his sense o' equilibrium.
Ensnared, within that web-site tight,
He clutched the desk to stay upright.
His right hand groped in frantic grips,
And couped a tray o' paper clips,
Ball point pens, the wee brass bell,
The tannoy microphone as well.
Then, to complete the tragic farce,
Ian fell among them on his arse!
Beside the printer, now black lacquered,
The hard disk was completely knackered.
The keyboard lay in fifty bits,
Liz swooned, and had a bout o' fits.

The insurance claim form came to school.
They heard the tale, then paid in full.
Ian's erudition is quite super,
He confessed in Latin: *Mea Culpa.*

Now wha this tale o truth shall read,
Ilk man and mother's son tak heed;
Modern technology's quite exciting,
Word processors improve your writing.
Spreadsheets do accounts with ease
You can work a laptop on your knees.
But the moral o' this wee bit fable
Is *cavete* a trailing cable!

CROCODILE
DUNDEE

I'm hearing bits o' gossip
Fae the wans that's in the know,
That Geordie Shearer's not the man
He was some time ago....

I landed in on Moira,
(George was oot) the other night ;
There's mischief in yon woman,
For she cried, "Oh, what a sight!"
For Moira misses nothing,
And she spied, with eagle eye,
That when I'd left the hoose that night
I hadnae zipped my fly!
And before I could compose mysel'
To make a wee bit pass,
She dived into a drawer
For a magnifying glass!
And on its box was printed,
"For the man who can't find it".
And she says that glass has cheered up
Geordie Shearer quite a bit!
For every time he uses it,
He feels it's proved its worth,
He believes there's no' a finer man
Exists in all the North!

Moira tells me Geordie's takin' her,
To the land they call, "Down Under".
He's bought a pair o' boxer shorts.
(That's sure to make ye wonder...
Is Geordie Shearer plannin'
For to hae a bit o' fun,
Wi' yon big Australian lassies
Wi' bikinis in the sun?)
Put a halter on him Moira,
For he's whispered it to me,
He thinks he's the Ardross version o'
Yon Crocodile Dundee!

I see Moira Shearer's laughing,
Ah well she'll laugh no more,
For her secrets are revealed
In this next wee bit o' lore!
She's a time o' it wi' Geordie,
Though he keeps her in fine style,
There's aye a trace o' mischief
In his enigmatic smile.
He bought her Christmas present,
One of his most extravagant ventures
Would ye believe it if I telt ye
Was a brand new set o' dentures?
So Moira dinna laugh too much
For though I have nae doot,
That your teeth are fittin' fine
There's just a chance.... they might jump oot!

TO DAVID INGLIS - CHIEF ENGINEER
On his 60th Birthday

For forty days and forty nights the rain came peltin' doon;
The tide was risin' fast roon' Noah's ark.
He'd gathered all the world's beasts and penned them all aboard
For things were really looking pretty dark.

There was only one mair problem left that Noah hadnae solved
For he grew up herding cattle, sheep and goats.
Now driving herds o' animals demands a lot o' skill,
But it's no' just quite the same as handlin' boats.

Though Shem and Ham and Japheth and their wives made up the crew,
Nane o' them had ever been afloat.
While Noah slept the angel o' the Lord appeared and said,
"Ye'll need an engineer to drive the boat.

"I've heard tell that up in Scotland there's a breed o' engineers
Wi' banes like piston rods and blood like ile,
If ye can get wan (and his wife) to keep this boatie runnin' fine,
Ye can cruise the world's oceans in fine style".

So Noah and his boys signed up a Clydeside engineer
Fae a tanker, lyin' at anchor in the bay;
Thanks to Noah's clever foresight there's been Scottish engineers
Manning engine rooms o' ships right to this day.

David Inglis is the offspring o' this hardy breed o' men;
He was born way back in 1938.
He was brocht up by his grannie and two formidable aunts,
In the style that made the British Empire great!

He got yokit tae his lessons, and he did no' bad at school,
Then he startit work in Polmaise Colliery;
Whene'er he'd served his time as an apprentice engineer,
Like his faither, he packed up and went to sea.

Wi' a monkey wrench in one hand, and a manual in the other,
A greasy bunnet sailin' close-hauled on his head,
He mastered diesel engines, steam-powered winches, lifting gear,
And his career was telegraphed at *Full Ahead.*

He crossed the world's oceans while he learned his noble trade,
And he quickly climbed from rank to rank each year;
Till, with four gold rings upon his sleeve, he joined that elite band,
Who can proudly call themselves *Chief Engineer.*

He cruised on as a bachelor till 1983,
Then an Irish lassie breezed into his life.
Her eagle-eye detected creases on his drip-dry, non-iron shirts,
And she thocht: "My lad, it's time you had a wife!"

He asked her what she liked to drink: " Glenmorangie", she said.
"Oh, that's great, for it's my favourite tipple too".
So he poured a gen'rous dram, and then another followed on;
Guess what came next?...Och well, I'll leave the rest to you.

Alpha -Victor - Foxtrot was the signal he sent out,
(The seaman's code for *Come Close By My Side*)
Sheila hoisted up *C Charlie*, the *Affirmative* reply,
And in 1987 became his bride.

Whenever this Chief Engineer takes leave and comes ashore
Wi' his greasy overalls all stained wi' lube,
He responds to *Full Ahead* or *Half Astern* just the same,
But it's Sheila's voice comes doon the speakin' tube!

And now he's reached his three-score years wi' engines runnin'fine,
He flies *Papa - Whisky - Golf* f'ae his cross-trees;
Vessel in Good Condition is the message it proclaims,
And there's nae doubt Sheila readily agrees!

WHODUNNIT

Now, here's some hot gossip that raised a wee smile
When it came to my ears... though it took a guid while!
It's a torrid wee tale o' a night o' romance
When a bold lad in here took an amorous stance.
Intent on impressing his ain heart's desire
He drove into the wood - for his loins were on fire.

Now... this tale's confidential, so I can't tell his name,
For he'd just hang his heid wi' black, burning shame!
I see three or four heids beginning to tilt -
There's a few lads in here wi' feelings o' guilt!

In the passenger seat, a shapely young miss,
Parted her lips in a passionate kiss.
Her soft, yielding flesh gave in to his charms,
As she melted, like snaw, in his powerful arms.
This rustic, inflamed by the fire in her lips,
Cast care to the winds and took haud o' her hips.
He cairted her in to the back o' the van,
Wi' miraculous strength - like the bionic man.
Consumed by desire and unfettered lust,
Oh Boy, they fairly raised up the dust!

No, I see ye're a' gaspin', but I have to say "No":
*I could never expose this **real** Romeo.*

Enraptured, engulfed in a storm tide o' bliss,
He had failed to take note, there was something amiss.
In his ardent desire for the love he had found,
He had parked his wee van on some very soft ground.
Wi' the weight in the back it sunk into the dubs
And was firmly embedded - right up to the hubs!

Now, I ken ye're a' curious, but ye'll just have to guess
The name o' the lad who got into this mess.

This gallant young buck then cast his love loose
To walk for two miles - in high heels - to a hoose
To telephone so she could get him some help,
But not before she had geid him a skelp.
She telt him outright that he was nae good,
Then she left him alone wi' his van in the wood,
The poor quine didnae ken which way she should go
Till she knocked on a door... and met auld Kate Munro
Who took the lass in and gave her some tea.
Thirty four years later... Kate let on tae me!

But the mystery remains who her lover-boy could be....
Don't worry Acky Davidson, your secret's safe wi' me!

BETTER LATE THAN NEVER

There's Bobby Lowe, now let me think,
Is Bobby on, or off, the drink?
He works so hard, I've heard it said,
One day, when he came home to bed
He had a dram, and then a snooze.
Well, maybe it was just the booze
That caused confusion when he woke
And saw the time, "Oh, Holy Smoke!"
He rushed to work with urgent haste,
There wasnae any time to waste.
He bought his paper at the shop
(His usual early morning stop).

Arriving at his work quite late,
He wondered when he saw the gate,
Was still locked up, but then his eyes,
Opened wide with great surprise.
Aye, right enough, poor Bob was late,
For on the paper was the date.
It gave poor Bobby such a fright,
He'd come back to work at eight at night!

Like Tam O Shanter, Bobby, think...
It's high time you gave up the drink!

DOCTOR'S ORDERS

George Morrison's blood pressure
Is the cause for some concern;
He went to see the doctor,
The cause of it to learn.
His diet's low in fatty foods,
There's nae cholesterol;
He eats greens and plenty roughage,
There's nae problem there at all.
He aye has plenty exercise,
And never takes a smoke,
But still the pressure's goin'up,
Nae kiddin', it's nae joke!

The doctor said, "There's naethin' wrang,
Unless it is the drink...
D'ye tak a dram or two?"
Said George, "Well doctor, let me think...
Occasionally... at weekends like,
I micht hae wan or two."
The doctor looked him in the eye,
"Is what ye're sayin' true?
For the wey your pressure's shootin'up,
Ye'll soon be off tae heaven..."
Said George, "Ah well, it's maybe more
Like five, or six, or seven".

At that the doctor said, "Aye, Aye,
My lad, cut doon by half!"
With that advice George blushed a bit,
And gave a nervous laugh.
"Weel, doctor, I'll be honest,
And come completely clean,
The number's mair like...
Let me see, a nice round...seventeen!"

So Geordie took the doc's advice,
To sort out all his troubles,
He's cut the number doon by half,
He now just orders doubles!

SURPRISE SURPRISE!

Presented to Donald McMillan on his marriage to Julie Simpson,
8th August 1992

Donald first came to life on a Sunday;
At tea time Katie was glum,
"I've got a wee pain,
Indigestion again."
At nine, she'd become Donald's Mum

He was aye a determined wee cratur,
And when his behaviour was bad,
His mother would flush
And voice her disgust
"He's just takin' efter his Dad!"

While abroad, he picked up some German,
At school, he learned French (wi' a stammer);
But the language was bad
That he learned from his Dad
When he hit his thumb wi' the hammer!

His Dad introduced him to culture;
To Burns and Shakespeare and Chaucer.
When his tea was too hot,
It was Daddy who taught
Him to drink it straight oot o' the saucer.

One night, he took up sleep-walkin';
His eyes had a wide glassy stare.
He walked o'er to my side,
His flies opened wide
And he piddled all over my chair.

Together we went fishing for lobsters;
He learned all the splices and knots.
But he made a mistake
When he stood in my wake
While I cleared my nose o' the snots.

A wee fish bone once poisoned his finger.
The penicillin injection was sore;
Not a tear did he weep,
Never uttered a cheep.
He passed oot in a heap on the floor!

He was always a fitness fanatic;
He exercised right to his limit.
Weight training was fun
But when it was done
He smelt like a peat-cutter's semmit.

When he first took an interest in lassies,
He was proud o' his manly good looks;
But it dented his charm
When to his alarm
He developed a fine crop o' plooks.

He fell in wi' this lassie ca'd Julie.
I can understand how he feels;
She's fit and she's strong
And he took her along
In the boat .... and she hauled the creels!

When he asked Nick's permission to marry
As a well-bred young man really ought-ter.
Nick said, "It's your life,
But have you seen the wife?"
He said, "Yes, but I fancy your daughter!"

Now Julie, you've come to know Donald
And that mischievous look in his eyes
Means on your wedding day
He's been scheming away
To bring you a special surprise.

For when Donald is faced with a problem
And doesn't know quite what to do,
He'll furrow his brow
And say, "Dad, show me how....."
So I'm booked for the honeymoon too!

DOWN IN THE DUMPS

Did ye read the New Year's Honours List? There were folk like you and me
That had been nominated to receive the OBE.
Fair play, there's some that earned it, but it fair gets up my hump
That they overlooked the heroes that man the Cooncil Dump.
We couldnae dae withoot the scaffies to lift the junk we a' throw oot
And the boys that work the dump deserve a medal, I've nae doubt.
So here's a poet's humble tribute - it's just a wee bit lore
About a legendary character, fae the dump there at Newmore.

A handsome, mighty, muscular man, wi' looks clean-cut and lean
Buries a' the rubbish wi' a mighty big machine.
This two hundred horse-powered monster, wi' its turbo-assisted booster
Is driven by local superman - Alistair Ross, the Rooster!

The Rooster handles his bulldozer wi' skill and dash and flair
And he doesnae mind a teeny bit the stench that's in the air,
For he kens there's aye rich pickings in the things that folk fling oot;
An auld rocking chair, a picture frame, or a single welly boot.
Its Sod's law that wan welly always bursts before the ither,
If ye pick up wan that's wholesome, then ye'll soon pick up its brither.
As he plouters in the glaur, his left boot's black and size thirteen,
The right boot's size eleven in a nice bright shade o' green.

He once gave Margaret some red roses, and her heart began tae thump,
"Oh Rooster, how romantic!" He said, "I found them in the dump".

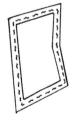

His eagle eye has spotted a Victorian threepenny bit,
A clutch o' blackthorn walking sticks, a wee bairn's dummy tit,
A silver tipped walking cane fae a country gent's big hoose,
A mangy set o' antlers fae an auld Canadian moose.
The pair o' thermal long drawers that warm the Rooster's rump
Were rescued fae a pile o' rags he found there at the dump.
I could go on all night an' tell ye o' this hero's great adventures -
Can ye guess now where the Rooster got his bottom set o' dentures?

One day when he was picking o'er the treasures o' the place,
He found a stringless violin in a battered leather case.
That night he took the fiddle oot, whenever he got hame,
Stamped on the back was Stradivarius, a familiar sounding name.
" I've heard that name before", said he, for he's no' withoot some culture,
Even though Acky Davidson says he's just a bloody vulture.
"This might be worth a pound or two", was his educated guess,
He gave the fiddle a wee bit wipe and then set off for Inverness.

The dealer saw him coming - "What's this ye've got?" says he,
And when he saw the Stradivarius, he rubbed his hands wi' glee.
He shouted to his henchman, working through the back himself,
"Aw Wullie - hoo mony Stradivarius violins have ye got there on the shelf?"
"Och dozens", cried back Wullie " There's nae demand for them at a".
The dealer shook his head, "I'll gie ye £50, that's a".

A week or two then passed: the Rooster had another find,
An oil painting in a gilded frame - I'm sure ye ken the kind.
When he dichted aff the stour on that ancient work of art,
And saw the signature was Rembrandt, he felt a thumpin' in his heart!

"This must be worth a bob or two", and off he went once more
To Inverness and marched right through the antique dealer's door.
"What's this ye've got the day then? That's a bonny picture frame".
"Aye, but look here at the signature; now that's a famous name.
Unless I am mistaken, this is a genuine auld master".
But the dealer showed his mettle, for his mind was working faster.

"Aw Wullie", cried the dealer, "Have ye ony Rembrandts through the back?"
"I'm tripping o'er the bloody things", he cried, "I could sell them by the sack".
"Ach weel then", said the dealer "I'll offer £50".
So the Rooster took the money wi' a disappointed frown.

Now our hero was suspicious that the rogues had ta'en him in,
But he resolved to get his ain back when he had a lucky win.
At the fun fair at the Games he won two coconuts and laughed,
"I'll show that pair o' rogues now that the Rooster isnae daft".

He took them in a plastic bag to the dealer once again.
"Whit's this ye've brought the day then," said the dealer in his den.
The Rooster lifted oot a coconut, " Now listen here, ma boy,
This is wan o' the bollocks aff the Wooden Horse o' Troy,
And before ye shout tae Wullie, let me tell ye loud and clear,
A horse has just **two** bollocks - and I've got the ither yin right here!"

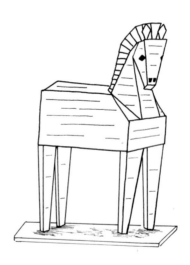

ECONOMICAL WITH THE TRUTH

The discovery of a very rare tree on the construction site of the Inverness Aquadome in 1996 by Urquhart Morrison brought multiple benefits. His employers and the press were delighted to demonstrate their concern for the environment, and Urquhart knows how to take advantage of such a situation.

Ye'll hear o' many queer-like capers
That get folks' names in a' the papers,
But I've never heard the likes o' yon -
Keen gardener - Urquhart Morrison?

Though Urquhart rates *The Sun* at zero,
The Sun made him a local hero.
It featured Urquhart on page three
For saving an exotic tree.

While working at a building site,
He brought this rarity to light.
It grew unknown to one and all,
Till Urquhart answered nature's call,
And crept into a leafy glade
Where he saw a twig above his head.
Each stalk had leaves distinctly varied;
One big, one small and slightly hairy'd.
Though he'd never been to University,
His arboricultural curiosity
Was aroused by these botanic freaks,
And, hitching up his wrinkled breaks,
He resolved to find this strange tree's name.
He reckoned this might bring him fame;
It might be of interest to the media.
He perused the gardening encyclopaedia
And sure enough his tree was there,
A cut leaf hornbeam, very rare!
Its botanical name he thought much nicer,
Carpinus Betula Incisa,
So, armed with scientific lore,
Urquhart went back to work once more.

Construction work next day was halted,
For Urquhart's find was now exalted.
An expert called up to the site
Declared his identification right.
Reporters came for interviews
And Urquhart's tree was front-page news.
The press men praised his acumen
In spotting this rare specimen
And modestly, they heard him tell,
"I'm keen on gardening masel'".

But Urquhart kens a story's worth,
And saving trees gi'es him a drouth.
They paid for Urquhart's front page yarn
Wi' a case o' Bold John Barleycorn!

Alison beamed, for she was prood
O' her wee man (the boy done good!)
Until she read the P & J
At breakfast time that Saturday.
She gasped... and sat richt sair astonished!
"Urquhart Morrison!" She then admonished:
"I'll gie ye credit, ye are a trier;
Ye're shameless and a barefaced liar!
'Keen gardener', ye've telt the P&J.
The truth is you dae sweet F.A.!"

But Urquhart gently hushed her cries,
"I wasnae really telling lies".
He supped a dram to slake his drouth,
"I was Economical wi' the Truth".

EPISTLE TO A FALLEN MAN

On hearing of Eddy Robberts' sixteen foot fall from the top of an unsecured ladder.

Fair fa' your honest sonsie face,
Ed. Robberts o' the great Dutch race;
I hear ye climbed up to a place
To shift some bales,
And fell with ill conceiv-ed grace
And mournfu' wails.

I'd hae thocht, aul frien', that you would show
Concern for safety when ye go
Cimbing ladders - you should know
To dae it richt.
A man should hang on doon below
To haud it ticht!

Your only thocht was D-I-Y,
When'er ye climbed that ladder high,
To knock doon bales to feed the kye,
A' by yersel.
But noo ye've learned the hardest wey -
For doon ye fell!

What man can fly doon through the air,
Land upon a concrete flair
And stay alive, though mighty sair?
But, in this farce,
What saved you was your landing gear -
A big, fat arse!

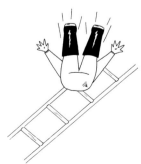

Ye landed wi a thund'rous thump,
Bounced twa-three times upon your rump,
Wan cheek swelled right up, like a hump
Upon a camel.
To walk wi' that lopsided lump
Was sic a trammel.

Ye hirpled hame in painfu' haze;
Left open gates in thoughtless daze.
Ye paid the price for errant ways
And silly sallies.
The cattle a' escaped to graze
Among the chalets!

Ye met auld Scott there in the toon,
(And he's anither crippled loon).
Wi' sticks, ye baith went limpin' roon;
Cried Scott, "B' Jesus,
We must get oot o' here real soon -
'fore McMillan sees us....!"

In spite o'poor auld Scotty's fears
Folk rang this bard, to fill his ears
Wi' gossip, laced wi' laughter's tears.
It's nae surprise;
Invergordon walls, as well as ears,
Have prying eyes!

The phone lines then began to hum;
The story swelled, like Eddy's bum.
The Rooster, then Ack, added some
Choice words as well
And what they said just left me numb -
I darena tell!

Steeped in your bath, a pained ablution
Wi' tender care in execution
For fear that multi-hued contusion
Was like to burst,
Ye made your New Year Resolution.
It's - Safety First!

ARTIFICIAL INSEMINATION

The wonders of veterinary science as seen through the eyes of a humble crofter.

Sex education's now a subject the bairns get at the school,
But Dennis learned the facts o'life observin' his old bull.
Inevitably, the time came when the poor beast passed away,
And left a love-sick heifer all forlorn and in dismay.

But Acky gave him some advice, a piece o' richt guid news,
"Artificial insemination's just the thing for randy coos.
Just phone up John Simpson, he's in the surgery the day".
So Dennis reversed the charges, and booked John right away.

John telt him, "Bring the heifer in and gie her plenty hay,
If I fail to get her pregnant then ye willnae have to pay".
Well, a bargain's aye a prisoner when Dennis Scott's aroon',
He'd never heard the likes o' yon, being a simple crofter loon.

He was just richt sair astonished; he kent vets had some schoolin',
But he really didnae think they'd had to take a course in bullin'.
So Dennis said to John as he came through the byre door:
"Just hing yer troosers on that nail - it'll keep them off the floor".

EPISTLE TO EWEN STEWART

To commemorate his retirement after thirty seven years of devoted service as Principal Teacher of Music in Invergordon Academy. His reputation as a choirmaster brought no fewer than four invitations to bring the school choirs to perform at St Giles Cathedral in Edinburgh.

Lament in rhyme, lament in prose;
The saut tears trickle doon my nose,
For Ewen Stewart's had his dose
O' education.
And blithely now he onward goes
To Superannuation.

Forget the jargon o' our schools,
Problem pupils, exam board rules;
Tho' honest nature made some fools
To fill your classes,
By dint o' your exceptional skills
They a' got passes.

For years, undaunted, ye wad ding
To mak a croakin' corbie sing,
Till blithe-like notes, ye'd gar to wring
By charm or ire.
By miracle or sic-like thing,
Ye'd hae a choir.

For choral singin' is your passion,
And tho' it's maybe oot o' fashion,
Ye've earned a noble reputation
For excellent choirs.
Your star still shines throughout the nation
And never tires.

Ye're quintessentially philharmonic;
Your quest for elegance in matters sonic,
Wi' sensuous rythms, diatonic,
Has brought ye fame.
To choristers ye seem demonic,
But that's your game.

Ye conduct a choir wi' awesome power;
Ye coax, cajole and sometimes glower
If wan false note comes floatin' ower -
Maist like fae me!
St Giles must be your finest hour;
It bears the gree!

Your repartee is unsurpass'd,
Your caustic wit has style and class;
Ye're partial to a gen'rous glass
O' malt, it's said.
I wonder that some comely lass
Ye ne'er ha'e wed?

A wheen o' lassies weel may miss ye,
And, in their dearest mem'ries place ye;
A puckle laddies too may bless ye,
Wi' tearful e'e.
For weel, I wat, they'll ne'er forget ye,
Until they die.

And here am I, a coof, and glaikit;
My education's sair negleckit.
I thocht that spoons were things ye lickit,
Till I came here.
Inspired by you, they now mak' music,
Tho' I play by ear.

But whiles ye've made me look a fool,
Wi' your tannoy announcements to the school;
Now, Shostakovitch sounds real cool -
And that's fair play.
But Dvorak breaks Phonetics' rule,
I have to say!

It's strange how nature's master plan,
Conceiv-ed sic a cultured man
And placed ye in the Stewart Clan!
(There's some that thinks
That a' the Stewarts in the lan'
Are nocht but tinks!)

Your work rate's showed nae *Rallentando*,
Ye've soldiered on withoot *Mancando*,
Nor e'en a hint o' *Tremolando*.
Ye're ne'er *Stacatto;*
Your life has been one grand *Crescendo*
Sempre Legato.

Here's blessings from this cheery gang,
Wha dearly like a jig or sang,
And though we may be richt or wrang
By music's rule;
Your mem'ry will be cherished lang
In this, *your* school.

EPISTLE TO THE ROOSTER

In 1996 the Rooster was presented with a framed poem honouring his work at the council dump. This seemed to have gone to his head with devastating consequences a few weeks later.

Hail to ye, Rooster! Ye were praised
Last year, in status highly raised.
A poet's tribute had ye dazed
Wi' words sae fine.
Or was it drink that left ye crazed
Hauf oot your mind?

For Rooster, wha wad hae expeckit
Your duty ye wad sae negleckit,
To leave the handbrake unconneckit
On your earthmover?
And gravitation then eleckit
To take things over.

And then began a woefu' tale.
The earthmover trundled doon the dale;
It'd ta'en a notion for a sail
On Stoneyfield Lake.
But it submerged - just like a whale -
Wi' frothing wake.

Three fathoms doon it came to rest;
And then began a muckle test
As cranes and divers a' did wrest
To haul it out.
Oor Council Tax will bear the cost,
I dinna doubt.

But we'll forgi'e ye o' your vice,
If ye buy us all a drink; the price
Will maybe teach ye to be wise.
Guid faith! That scared ye!
And mind, watch oot for slippy ice,
When fu' at Ne'erday!

Auld frien', in here we think nae ill
O' lads like you (wha tak a fill),
And if, perchance, misfortune will
Again befall;
Keep mind that Pride (so often) comes
Before a Fall.

Acky Davidson
*Expressions that ladies
would not understand*

Mrs Allison
No' built for exercise

Urquhart Morrison
Keen gardener

Dennis Scott
Nae man on earth that's as tight!

*Three hundred tons o'
prime sewage in a
field doon at
Lower Kincraig*

John McMillan
A rhymer like by chance

Eddy Robberts
Speaks English much better than Ack

George Morrison
Just orders doubles

A MAN LIKE HIS DAD

Presented to Euan McMillan on his marriage to Carol MacLeod - 7th September 1990

Euan sprang into life out in Germany,
I mind it as clear as can be,
At quarter past six on a Monday,
He arrived just in time for his tea!

He was always a cheerie wee chappie,
Aye smilin', nae tantrums nor howls,
If ye let him eat like a maggot.
Aye... he aye had a good set o' bowels!

At school, he strolled through his studies,
Exam results were....well, no' too bad.
He could never get off wi' his mischief;
It's tough when the teacher's your Dad.

The first time he dated a lassie,
He took pride in how he would look,
A new hair style to make him look classy,
And Mum's make up covered a plook.

He fancied his chances that evening,
And tried to get fresh bye and bye,
Wi' wan o' yon awkward first kisses,
Where each got a nose in the eye.

He got into yon terrible music,
Like most teenage lassies and boys;
They go into the discos to boogie,
And they come oot deaf wi' the noise.

At Tullich, in a ramshackle caravan,
He came to Lochcarron to live;
'Twas infested in summer wi' midges,
In the winter it leaked like a sieve.

He tackled his housework wi' gusto,
Made the bed, washed the dishes, and then,
Round about ....seven months later,
He'd start all over again.

The lavy was something quite special,
A tiny wee portable loo;
Whenever he ran out of paper,
A handful of dockens would do.

At that time he got awfu' hairy;
His head sprouted long flowing locks.
It looked like Lochcarron at low tide,
When the tangle just hings on the rocks.

Some time passed and then he met Carol;
She smoothed out the kinks in his life,
So it isn't really surprising,
That she's now sitting here as his wife.

Now Carol, I'm sure ye'll be hoping,
That the kind of man you have wed,
Is considerate, good-humoured and handsome,
And he'll bring ye your breakfast in bed.

To exotic locations for holidays,
He'll take ye to some far-off place;
Like, o'er the minches to Uist,
Where the wind blaws the sand in your face.

He'll help ye to carry the shopping,
And gie ye a hand wi' the dishes;
He'll provide ye wi' food for your table,
A feast o' yon big salmon fishes.

He'll play wi' the bairns when your busy;
Walk the dog, and see that it's fed.
He'll get up to change the bairn's nappies
In the night, while you lie in your bed.

He'll never forget to buy presents
That'll bring a wee smile to your face.
He'll jump at the chance if ye let him,
Put a fresh lick o' paint on your place.

Intelligent, affectionate, generous,
Without a word o' a lie
If he'd been born a year or two sooner,
He'd 've been snapped up by yon Princess Di!

Aye, Carol, ye can count yersel' lucky
To have captured a promising lad;
For if Euan turns out like I've told ye....
He'll be just a man like his Dad!

AN ILL WIND

The use of sewage sludge to fertilise the fields of Lower Kincraig and an industrial dispute over the withdrawal of free orange juice for welders at the oil rig fabrication yard of Highlands Fabricators at Nigg in the mid-1980s sets the scene for the events accurately chronicled, with only a hint of poetic licence, in these verses.

Acky stopped one day by the garden,
To yarn for a while at the dyke,
And he told me how he had scuppered,
A dispute called, "The Orange Juice Strike".

Well, it seems that the unions and pickets,
Had been planning for half o' the night,
To drive on the A9 in convoy,
To beseige the Hi-Fab Nigg Site.

A double decker bus, filled wi' polis,
Joined in lest there might be some trouble,
But what they had all failed to reckon,
Was on Davidson burning his stubble.

Wi' the scent o' blood in their nostrils,
They sped on for all they were worth,
But the wind then changed its direction,
Veering South - it had started fae North.

So it blew a' the reek fae the stubble
In dense clouds right o'er the road,
And when Acky caught sight o' the convoy,
He cried oot in a panic, "Oh, Goad!"

When the convoy sped into the smoke screen,
There was an almighty great crash,
And Acky said, "Gosh" and "Good Gracious!"
For he'd never seen such a stramash!

To be honest, he used some expressions,
That the ladies would not understand,
For Acky's peculiar phrasing,
Is unique in the whole o' the land.

But that cloud had its own silver lining,
For no one was injured or maimed,
And the drivers all bought themselves new cars,
Off the insurance, whenever they claimed.

And soon they forgot the bit trouble,
About the withdrawal o' juice,
For all their attention was focussed,
On the gleamin' new cars by the hoose.

So, the Orange Juice Strike was extinguished,
Thanks to Acky, the wind and the smoke,
And the incident passed into legend,
And became a bit o' a joke.

But 10 Downing Street heard the story,
And a letter was posted to Ack,
"Ye're a hero, ma loon", wrote Maggie,
"Ye deserve a wee pat on the back".

"We'll mak ye a knight o' the realm,
Or gie ye a seat in the 'Lords'".
Well Acky was richt sair astonished,
And for once, he was near stuck for words!

Now, the thocht o' the title, 'Sir Acky',
To be fair, it appealed for a while.
But parliamentary language?
That's really no' quite Acky's style!

"Dear Maggie", he wrote in his letter,
"I acknowledge the praises you've sung,
But actually, I wad prefer it,
If you'd send me some bogies o' dung".

Now the bogies o' dung are arriving,
Fae the North, South, the East and the West,
So now ye ken why Acky's barley,
Is always graded the best.

But when Acky is spreading his sewage,
There are some who express discontent,
For the atmosphere round Invergordon,
Takes on a peculiar scent.

There's a moral in every good story,
And I think it is well understood,
That the moral in this one, is clearly,
"It's an ill wind blaws naebody good".

AEROBICS

(Strange goings-on in Ardross Village Hall)

I've a neighbour who's a sportsman,
His quarry is the *Famous Grouse*,
And he plucks them off their perches,
In the local public house.
Wan nicht, he'd had a brace or two,
(The sport was mighty pleasin'),
His collies had to guide him home,
For ye micht say, he was bleezin'.

But the village hall attracted him,
Though his heid was sorely goupin',
For there were goin's on, a-goin' on,
Wi' sounds like grunts and loupin'.

He crept roon' tae the windae;
He was already on all fours
And he couldnae reach the handles
To come in through the doors.

'T was an unco sicht that met his eyes -
A pechin', heavin' mass -
The Women's Rural Institute,
At their ladies' keep-fit class!

They'd cast off all their knittin',
And put by their wee bit sewin',
And set to with dedication,
To look like Pamela Ewing.
Their tweed skirts, brogues and overcoats,
Were strewn about at random,
In leotards and stre-e-e-tch tutus,
They pranced with gay abandon.

Except for Mrs Allison,
She stood weel tae the side:
"I'm no' built for exercise",
In a plaintive voice she cried.
"If I slim doon ma hurdies,
Like the rest o' you auld freeks,
I'd have to get my clubbie book
And order brand new breeks!"

THE ARDROSS LASSIES

A Toast to the Lassies: Ardross Burns Supper 1988

Ye've heard that Rabbie Burns was a lad o' many parts,
Though he left us poems and songs, he left a trail o' broken hearts.
For maist folk ken him as a lad who made a wheen o' passes,
That seldom failed to win the hearts o' hauf o' Ayrshire's lassies.
In spite o' a' that writing, aye, a hundred thousand words,
He was equally prolific when it came tae pullin' birds!
A fermer chiel, he sowed his seeds o' barley, neeps and oats,
But he scattered ither seed aboot - count his weans - aye, lots and lots!
Though he died in abject poverty, if he'd waited just a while,
The family allowances would've kept him in fine style.
Family planning back in Rabbie's day
Was , "Ae Fond Kiss and then we sever".
The doctor now prescribes "the Pill", and then ye're safe for ever!

Have ye noticed in the modern books and the plays that's on TV
That the lassies are much mair brazen than in bygone days they'd be?
Rab would stand richt sair astonished, wi' envy he'd turn green
If he could get his hands on this month's Playboy magazine.
Now, I hear there is an auld wives tale, and I think it could be right,
That just a bit too much o' yon can be damaging to your sight.
(At this point the author hurriedly removed his spectacles!)
But the doctors say that healthy sex, your life it will prolong,
So now we know the secrets of Davie, George and Willie John,
While up there in Strathrusdale, where there's not much else to do,
Ritchie Martin is living proof that what the doctors say is true!

Now there's lassies driving juggernauts, and lassies driving stirks,
There's lassies dressed like ministers and they're preaching in the kirks.
Lassie doctors to tend your achin' banes, if ye suffer fae rheumatics,
And there's lassies wi' the figures to teach weans mathematics.
There's lassie fitba' players, some lassies wield a cricket bat,
Have ye seen the England cricket team? I'll say no more on that!
There's an Aberdeen lassies rugby team, every wan a richt good looker,
But they play wi' only fourteen....nae decent lass would be a "hooker".
There's lassies on the Cooncil and when they speak ye'll find,
That the lass that talks aboon them a' is.... Cooncillor Mrs Rhind!

Female intuition is a trait, in lassies it is strong.
It means that they are always right - even when we know they're wrong.
In the sales they'll go and buy things they don't need, but they'll say then,
They've spent a hundred and fifty pounds but have really saved you ten!
Some lassies cook yon foreign foods, like curries and chapatis,
But lads, like me, prefer a lass who'll gie them mince and tatties.
Some lassies have a husband, and there's some take two or more,
For some it's just a hobby, like yon lass Zsa Zsa Gabor.

But among the country's lassies, the Ardross lassies match the best,
(Even though it's only recently Ebe Foster passed her test).
There's the likes o' Janice Robertson who lives by writin' books,
And a multitude o' Mardons who are noted for their looks.
Nancy Kinloch there can charm a lad wi' foreign conversations,
Oak Cottage whiles attracts them fae the whole United Nations.
And there's Marge, wi' ruddy health she glows fae eatin'wholesome foods,
And Mairead sings in Gaelic, while she's busy paintin' nudes.
Sue Anderson's a strappin' lass that runs the Castle stable,
But steady boys, at handlin' frisky stallions she is able.
To be fair, there are some lassies, wi' a tongue as sharp's a razor,
But Davie says, "Oh no, ye can't be meaning Margaret Fraser".
Pauline's an enterprisin' lass. I'm sure ye must all know,
That she is now the Queen Bee o' the Ardross GPO.
I hear she's offerin' discount when ye go to tax your car,
And business is fair boomin', folk arrive fae near and far.
They spend their pensions buying petrol and a nice wee cup o' tea,
And Pauline's cash flow's put the twinkle back in Roddy's e'e.
There's Wilma wi' her herd o' goats that ranks among the best,
That's why the air is tainted when the wind veers roon' Nor' west!
The Avon Lady likes Strathrusdale, aye, the lassie isnae silly,
Her income's mair than doubled thanks to Wilma's famous billy!
Aboot the lassies in the Rural, we're unanimous in our views,
That if ye're lookin' for some gossip, they're the wans that have the news.

They say that Mrs Allison, (and it's mair than just a rumour),
Has been lately on a diet, to put a stop to my cruel humour
About her famous breeks that get an airin' here each year,
So here's a wee bit gossip that's been whispered in my ear.
She's turned vegetarian... suppin' rice and yon chapatis;
She's cut oot plates o' stew and has forsaken Stittenham tatties!
Her supper now consists o' just a pair o' lettuce leafs,
And she sits there lookin' sylph-like in a pair o' teeny briefs!
But when winter's icy blast attacks her tender loins, I ken,
Those cosy long-legged bloomers will see service once again!
They're functional and spacious and whenever there's a breeze,
She's glad she gets protection from the elastic at the knees.

Black burnin' shame upon you lads! At the auction in the hall,
For the value put upon a lass, who'd be at your beck and call,
Rachel Clarke was offering services to the lad that bid the most,
For two hours dedication to the wishes of her host.
But sadly for the hall roof fund, the lads were rather thrifty,
And the biddin' only reached the meagre sum of four pounds fifty!
It might've been much better to put an ANTIQUE auction on,
For the lassies would bid much mair for Davie, George and Willie John!
Yonder's Davie Oag of Dalmore... to him the lassies yield,
(He's weel kent as a farmer who's outstanding in his field!)
There's nae doubt he's a handsome chiel, the lassies all agree,
I once saw his charm in action at another Burns Soiree.
Wan lassie fascinated him till he couldnae wait nae mair,
So he summoned a' his rustic charm and strode oot o'er the flair,
"Lass, ye've got the biggest pair..... o' hands I've ever seen",
Well, the lassie was so flattered to be greeted like a queen,
And graciously acknowledged all the praises he had sung,
Then he said, "Wi' hauns like that.... ye could dae a turn at grapin' dung!"

When first I came to Ardross, I was a bashful lad, and shy,
I blushed when faced wi' lassies, and was aye tongue-tied forbye,
But I've learned a lot fae Davie, and the likes o' Willie John,
Who still can catch a lass's eye, even though he's gettin' on!
I share Willie John's opinion: Highland lassies are the best
And the lassies fae Ardross are surely leading a' the rest.

THE MATADOR

Let me tell you all a story :
One day when I met Ack,
He was wearing, on one foot, a training shoe.
On the other just as normal,
Was his usual wellie boot,
Says I, "There must be something wrong wi' you".

Then Acky told me of a mishap,
That had happened one fine day,
After Eddy had called Acky on the phone.
He'd a heifer that was randy
And he didnae have a bull,
Said Ack, "I'll let ye have my Charolais on loan".

So Acky hitched the trailer up,
And went to Dalnacloich,
Where he'd left two bulls to sort out who was boss.
Acky thought that in a day or two
They'd settle down just fine,
But when he got there both the bulls were feeling cross.

They were snorting at each other,
Then with heads down they would charge,
And the clash o' heads just rang out like a bell.
Then with malice they would glower,
Then they'd have another go,
And Acky said some words like, "Oh, well, well".

Then he cried out, " Stop ye're fechtin' boys,
It's time to go to work".
But the bulls replied with yet another thump.
Now patience is a virtue
That Acky hasnae got,
And he said, "I'll come and kick ye on the rump".

Now Acky is a hero,
And without a single thought
For his safety, and without a trace of fear,
He scaled the gate, and cried "Ole",
And strode into the fray,
While the divots fairly whistled past his ear.

Then Ack, the merry matador,
Let out a roar again,
"Ye silly beggers, will ye stop this flamin' farce!",
And when the bulls ignored his passioned plea,
For peace, goodwill on earth,
Acky joined in, wi' a kick to one bull's arse.

For an instant, this distraction
Gave the Limousin a chance,
Full astern the Charolais was forced to go.
Acky wasnae quite as nimble
As yon matadors in Spain,
And the bull reversed right on to Acky's toe!

Now Acky said a prayer,
Or some words to that effect,
Through clenched teeth there came a muffled kind o' sound
There was nae wey he could get his foot
From underneath its hoof,
It was already near six inches underground.

Somebody up there must have heard him,
For a chance soon came along,
As the Charolais regained a bit of way,
It stepped forward, Ack dived sideways,
Then rolled over in the mud,
And was free to live and fight another day.

Then the boys rushed in and grabbed him,
As he scrambled to his feet,
And helped him limp his way back to the car,
And they dabbed him wi' their hankies,
To remove the dark brown glaur,
For he looked just like an oversized Mars Bar.

Acky's foot was throbbing sorely,
As he pulled off his right boot,
It was swollen and a gaudy shade of blue.
So they took him to the doctor,
Who just smiled, and said to Ack,
"Now wasn't that a silly thing to do?"

But Acky is a hardy chiel,
The pain was quite severe,
And it was clear that Acky wasnae makin' on.
The x-ray showed no broken bones,
Just bruisin' and a sprain,
But the poor soul couldnae get his boot back on.

So he went and bought some trainers,
That would fit his tender hoof,
But just wore one, and then he hirpled up the street,
So that folk were sure to notice something odd,
And say to Ack,
"What's this, has something happened to your feet?"

Now I've a present here for Acky,
For an erstwhile matador,
It's certainly a gift that really suits.
It's just what Acky needs
For when he's fightin' bulls again,
A pair of sturdy, steel toe-cappit boots!

Most problems can be solved in a variety of ways, the solution often depending on the experience of the individual. Here are some innovative solutions which demonstrate a high level of lateral thinking.

TAKE UP THE SLACK

Now, if ye ever should need a good mason,
Let me give ye a bit o' advice.
Arthur Scott is the best in the district
And he charges a reasonable price.

One day, when Joan went oot shoppin'
She said, "Arthur, now when I come back,
I want to hang oot some washin'
But the claes line's a wee bittie slack".

Now to put ye all in the picture,
If ye'll bide a wee whilie wi' me,
This line ran oot fae the gable,
And o'er to an auld cherry tree.

Arthur's good at working out problems,
Wi' his bricks and mortar and trowel,
And so he devised a solution,
That's sure to make ye all howl.

For Arthur had solved the wee problem,
And left the job all nice and neat.
To tighten up Joan's wee bit claes line,
He moved the gable-end o'er three feet!

SPECIAL OFFER

Auld Scott has a nice wee bit croftie,
It's a real productive wee place.
He'll sell you a bag o' guid tatties,
But they're cheaper in Safeway or Mace.

If you're trying to learn to be thrifty,
Auld Scotty will teach you alright,
For Acky Davidson telt me,
"There's nae man on earth that's as tight!"

So auld Scott put an Ad. in the paper,
Just to prove that Acky was wrong.

A FREE BAG O' TATTIES

TO PENSIONERS!

(If they bring their Grannies along)

Some people need a little help from others to solve problems

ROYAL FLUSH

(Lines composed to commemorate a notable vist to the Smithfield Show)

The Smithfield Show's a big event in every farmer's year,
They scart the dung fae aff their boots, put on their smartest gear.
My neibor, Acky Davidson, in common wi' the rest,
Takes an annual holiday to go and see the best
In livestock and machinery, and meet the boys for crack,
But one year, let me tell you, there was a treat in store for Ack!

He slipped a fiver to Maureen, and said, "Now gie yersel' a treat,
The shops'll soon be open if ye wander doon the street.
I've arranged tae meet a crony while the stock judge picks the winner;
I'll meet ye later at the chip shop where I'll treat ye tae yer dinner".

Now Acky telt me this himsel', though I've written it in verse,
"The crowd o' folk was thick as flees aboot a bullock's erse!"
Wi' his hands stuck in the pockets o' his Marks and Spencer suit,
He muttered, forcing through the throng, " Whit's a' this fuss aboot".

As he scanned the crowd to see his freen, he saw a wee bit space,
An' thocht, "If I get o'er there, I'll maybe see his face".
A few steps mair, undaunted, Acky elbowed past a bobby
And bumped into a wifie who has farming for a hobby.

The wifie turned to Ack, smiled, and said, "Hello".
Said Acky, unabashed, "Aye, Aye, yer face I'm sure I know,
But let me think, yer name now...... it just escapes my mind".
But he took the hand she offered, while her name he tried to find.

Just then, the man escorting her, turned round wi' a grin,
And Acky gasped as if a coo had kicked him on the shin.
" Bloody Hell!" He cried out, "What a fool I've been!
That man's the Duke of Edinburgh... and you're the bloody Queen!"

- 56 -

And, of course, there's always the chance of help from ...

A MAN'S BEST FRIEND

One night, when duty called me
To a wee bit celebration,
I'd supped a dram or two,
With scant regard for Moderation.

Without too much embellishment,
It was really quite a binge,
And the thocht o' Katie's welcome
Was enough to make me cringe.

When I crept home in the early hours,
I was already on all fours,
So it wasnae just too easy,
To get in through the doors.

In the darkness o' the bedroom,
Katie turned roon' in her sleep,
So I quickly pressed my cauld wet nose,
(it had a wee bit dreep),
Against her hand and licked it,
Then she fondled roon' my lug,
And she fell back into slumber,
For she thocht I was the dug!

And when all else fails there's always....

THE POWER OF PRAYER

An auld wifie that bides in a croftie,
By the road that goes o'er Struie Hill,
When the Reverend MacDonald came calling,
Was lookin' a wee bittie ill.

When the minister speired why she was ailin',
It transpired, the laird wanted mair rent,
But it had been a bad year for the harvest,
And her income was already spent.

"Just trust the Guid Lord", said the minister,
As she made him his wee cup o' tea;
And when they had supped the refreshment,
He got down on the rug on his knee.

And he prayed to his maister in heaven,
To spare the auld wifie fae grief;
Then he left her wi' some words o' comfort,
That the Guid Lord would bring some relief.

When he called back, a day or two later,
There was nae sign o' grief nor o' strife.
She was struttin' aboot like a bantam,
Possessed o' a new lease o' life!

"Mr MacDonald, come in till I tell ye!
God's the boy, right enough. He took heed
O' what ye said in your prayers,
For the next day the laird drappit deid!"

TARRED AND FEATHERED

All that glitters is not gold

Acky Davidson's a humble man,
I'm proud to call my friend.
He plays life's game by knowing the rules,
And just how far they can bend.
He's always ready to take a risk,
If it earns him an extra buck,
But, whenever things go wrong,
He'll say some words ...that rhyme with duck!

I read this story in the Sunday Mail,
So I know it must be true.
I then got it straight from the horse's mouth,
And the air turned electric blue,
When Ack told me how misfortune fell,
The swear words rent the air,
As I heard how a cowboy tar gang
Conned an East Ross millionaire.

They arrived one day in the month of May
With a load of tar and chips,
When they saw the state of Ack's concrete road
They grinned and licked their lips.
"We've been doing some work on the council roads,
But there's tar to spare", said they:
"It'll have to be dumped if we don't find a home
 For what we've left today".

"When we saw the holes in your concrete road,
We thought you'd maybe feel
That, just for the price of materials,
We could maybe do a deal.
For £400 we'll tar and chip,
Fifty metres of road right here",
Said a man with a clip-on-badge on his coat
That said 'project engineer'.

To be fair to Ack, it seemed all above board,
And he didn't have time to wait,
With a bargain dangling in front of his nose,
He quickly rose to the bait.
"Fair enough", said he, rubbing hands with glee,
"But I'm off to a funeral soon.
Just go ahead and I'll settle up
At the end of the afternoon".

But when Ack returned to Lower Kincraig,
He was in for big surprise;
When he saw the job that the gang had done,
He couldn't believe his own eyes.
He gazed at 400 metres of road,
All tarred and covered in chips;
The 'project engineer' approached,
A sardonic grin on his lips.

"We've done you a favour", the boss man said,
As Ack gaped at the acres of tar.
"When the first bit of road was all spruced up,
The rest looked well below par.
So we reckoned you'd like us to finish the job,
And leave it all tidy and nice;
Now we're ready to go and oh, by the way,
£3000 is the price!"

Ack's eyebrows shot up, and his jaw dropped down;
It was clear that he wasn't impressed.
When he spoke to the 'project engineer',
His eloquence was up to the test.
He suggested a self-copulatory act,
For he's never been known to be stuck
A politically correct translation might be,
"I'm afraid you're clean out of luck."

Up lumbered a Frankenstein lookalike then,
And he grinned with a menacing leer;
He showed his finesse, as tobacco stained teeth
Bit the top off a bottle of beer.
His cheek had a scar from his ear to his mouth,
His chin was unshaven and furry;
And Ack couldn't stand the smell of his breath,
For he'd just had a take-away curry.

He weighed two hundred and fifty five pounds,
Stood well over six-foot-three.
He said: "You son of a gun, if you wanna have fun,
Well, that's OK by me".
His eyes had a cold, malevolent glint;
And he snarled, with a rasping sound,
"Would you like to see that barn up there,
Completely burned to the ground?"

Then a hand like a ham, with a vice-like grip,
Twisted Gordon's arm up his back.
And he growled, "I'll break your son's jaw for a start",
If there was any more lip from Ack.
Ack reckoned that this was a time to play smart,
Fair play, he'd just had a scare:
"Haud oan, noo", cried Ack, and he let fly a fart,
And it certainly helped clear the air!

Diplomatic activity resolved the dispute;
Acky haggled and knocked the price down.
He'd had to steer a safe course at the time,
But it cost him a cool thousand poun'.
Then the story got out and the papers got in,
And they published the facts fair and square,
And the whole world then knew how the tar gang had conned
A now-famous East Ross millionaire.

But alas for poor Ack, there was more to come out;
When the quarrymen told the tale,
How they'd fiddled the weight when the gang came for chips,
To add twenty per cent on the sale.
So the quarry boys had conned the cowboys who'd conned
Poor Ack out of £1000.
At least he could say that his folly that day,
Helped the wheels of commerce go round.

But before you begin to laugh at poor Ack,
Just think where he got his cash.
He gets subsidies for less favoured land,
Where there's nothing but peat bogs and rash.
He coins in a premium on oil seed rape,
And barley, and wheat, and for flax,
And then there's a grant for land set aside -
And it all comes from our income tax!

Farmers just can't survive in this day and age,
On the income from livestock or crops;
It's merely a pittance compared with the price,
Of the produce on sale in the shops.
So Ack feathers his nest with government grants,
To keep his bank balance steady.
But compared to the rest, he's still second best,
To that hairy-faced Dutchman called Eddy!

THE SHEEP TICKS O' STRATHRORY

In painful memory of a summer hillwalk in 1985 - wearing shorts

Burns wrote aboot the daisy,
And the toothache and the mouse,
And yon lodger in the lass's heid,
The blastit creepin' louse.

But if Rabbie went a-wandering
On the slopes o' Struie Hill',
The sheep ticks there would exercise
His literary skill.

They lurk among the heather;
They stalk ye thro' the grass!
They'll outjump any fleas alive,
If travellers dare to pass.

They attack in hordes like midges,
And they'll crawl inside your breeks;
They'll stick their heids right through your skin
And suck your blood for weeks!

Lassies, dinna wear a mini-skirt!
Boys, the kilt's oot for a start,
Or ye'll get an infestation
In your very private parts!

Yon's a vicious clan o' sheep ticks
That bide up in Strathrory,
At every General Election,
They come oot, and all vote Tory!

Maggie Thatcher is their Patron Saint,
They worship her, devout;
For, like a tick, she's hangin' on
And we cannae get her out!

TOP GUN

Lines dedicated to Urquhart Morrison, renowned story-teller,
and patron of the Old Dutch Barn

On a freezing day in winter
Wi' fresh sna' on the ground,
Urquhart went oot stalking
Wi' his gun and trusty hound.

He spied a stag up on the hill
An' stalked it through the sna'.
He shot the beast right through the heart,
Fae quarter a mile awa'!

The majestic beastie tumbled doon
The slope, where sna' was loose,
And, like a sna' ba', grew in size,
Till it looked as big's a hoose!

It thundered doon the corrie,
Till it hit a great big rock
And when Urquhart made his way doon there
He got a mighty shock!

For, in the remnants o' that sna' ba'
Lay his stag, but mair nor that....
Two hares, five rabbits, three grouse, a fox,
Four weasels and a cat!

There's no' a man alive
Could match the bag that Urquhart got,
An' ev'ry creature in it
Came fae only just wan shot!

This story grows, (just like the sna' ba'!),
Each time Urquhart tells his yarn,
When the drams are bought by tourists
Who frequent the Old Dutch Barn!

THE RUT

For Eddy, 94 has been a good year
He's fiddled his taxes and watered the beer;
The chalets are full, as folk keep coming back
And he even speaks English much better than Ack.

His son, Ernst, can certainly hold his head high,
But that's mainly because o' the length o' his thigh.
He was always a lad who lived without fear
Until an event that happened last year....

Now Ernst was a lad who happened to brag
He had nothing to fear fae that big rutting stag
Eddy keeps wi' the hinds in his ain wee bit zoo.
But let me assure you, Ernst kens better noo!

He went in one day to gie them their feeds,
But a stag in the rut has mair pressing needs!
It mistakenly thocht that Ernst had in mind
A torrid affair wi' a shapely young hind.

So the fun then got off to a real flying start
The stag let oot a roar, and a belch, and a fart.
Its antlers were lowered in an attitude such
As to tear oot the heart o' poor Ernie's crutch.

Ernst jooked and he jumped as he tried tae escape,
Like a toreador - but minus the cape -
While the stag tried to pierce his retreating behin'
Till at last he sought refuge behind a stout pine.

Now Ernst is a lad who's not without spunk.
As the stag wrapped its antlers around the tree trunk,
He grabbed hold o' its horns and held on real tight
And prayed that his bowels would withstand all the fright.

Then he cried oot tae Eddy, "I ken I'm a dope,
But Daddy come quickly and bring a bit rope".
Wi' the antlers tied on to the trunk of the tree,
They escaped to the hoose for a nice cup o' tea.

Now Ernie had scarcely got all his breath back
When who should arrive at the door - it was Ack!
Nae pity fae him - he thought it was funny,
And spotted a chance for makin' some money.

Eddy quickly latched on, for he saw a good chance
For free advertisin'... on TV.... for the Ranch.
"You've Been Framed" would pay for a home video
So he grabbed the camcorder, "C'mon Ernst, lets go".

"Repeat the performance and you'll be a star!
We can show it to customers here at the bar".
But Ernst cried he'd have none of this dangerous farce
"I don't want an antler rammed right up my arse!"

NAE BALLS AT ALL

While oot walkin' the dogs one evening,
I met Acky and stopped for a news,
And I heard o' the poor price for barley,
And the problems he had wi' his coos.
Says I, "Man, ye're lookin' gey weary,
Ye're a' peely-wally and white".
Says he, "It's this f-frightful wedding,
It keeps me awake every night".
Now Lorna, his dochter, is bonny;
She's engaged tae young Dougie MacKay,
And Acky's harrassed wi' arrangements,
For the wedding one day in July.
So I telt him a tale to amuse him,
As the poor soul was feelin' quite low,
For a frisky young stirk had just kicked him,
In a delicate place doon below.

There once was a couthy auld fermer
Whose dochter, (he only had wan),
Had never been blessed
Wi' the kind o' good looks
That wad let her get haud o' a man.
Wan year, wi' a bountiful harvest,
Invitations were sent out to all
The young lads and lassies to gather
In his barn to ha'e a grand ball.

The auld man was secretly hopin',
That this way some promisin' lad,
Wad be caught by his spinsterly dochter,
But och, things remained just as bad.
Well, the next year the ball was repeated,
Despite the expense to himself,
But still, at the end o' the evening,
The lassie was left on the shelf.

When, the third year, the lassie expected
A chance for a lad once again,
The auld man was less entertaining,
And telt her a thing aboot men,
He gave vent to his pent-up frustration
And said, "Lassie, now listen to me,
If ye can't get a man wi' two balls,
Ye'll never get wan wi' three!"

Said Ack, "Well, I havenae that problem",
And says he, (and I'll quote ye it all),
"For Lorna is such a braw lassie,
She got a man wi' nae balls at all!"

THE DISPLENISHMENT SALE

In memory of friends in Ardross

As I stretched oot by the fireside
A night or two ago,
The memories all came flooding back,
In the cosy hearthside glow,
Of the friends I've left behind me
Up the hill there in Ardross:
Aye, ever since I left the place
I've felt a sense o' loss.

There were days o' storm and power cuts
When to work I couldnae go -
I couldnae find the car
For it was buried in the snow!
But then that trusty auld green mini-bus
Came slidin' roon' the bend;
Fraser's Taxi alway runs on time
On that ye can depend!

Hot days, wi' just ma semmit on
At the Stittenham summer dippin'
And my back is no' the same
Since I was at the Crannich clippin'!
There were tasty Stittenham tatties,
Juicy neeps fae George Mackay;
I shut my eyes and thocht o' yon,
And fell asleep forbye.

And I dreamed o' folk fae Ardross
O' their character and style,
For I was at a displenishment sale
And I couldnae help but smile.
For though the pens were full o' livestock,
I tell ye, it's nae joke,
When I looked closely at their features,
They all resembled Ardross folk!

Anthony Walker caught a lot o' eyes
He was a bonny tup.
In fact, in the rare breed section,
It was him that won the cup!
"Ye'll find him very thrifty,
He's been runnin' on the hill".
The auctioneer's voice sang out,
"When he's ready for the kill,
Ye'll find no artificial hormones
In his diet, never fear,
And ye'll earn a hefty income
If ye clip him twice a year!"

"Now if you're the kind o' farmer
Whose purpose is specific,
To increase your production
There's a blood line here prolific.
On any kind of pasture,
Even heather on the moor
This pure bred flock o' Mardons
Is the best yet, that's for sure!"

Now the next pen had a big black beast,
"If ye're lookin' for an ox
For ploughin, cairtin neeps or dung,
Ye'll find this boy's the tops".
Though he'd lost some teeth
There was interest,
For the crowd around was thick;
His ain mother would've claimed
That it was surely big Bob Dick!

A pen o' three fine breedin' bulls,
Man, what a sight to see!
Broad shoulders, weel shaped rumps,
A frisky look was in their e'e.
Well the biddin' was intense,
I've never seen the likes o' yon!
But then these bulls had a' the features
O' Davie, George and Willie John!

Just then I met ma neebor,
Acky Davidson, f'ae doon the hill.
When it comes to judgin' livestock
There's few can match his skill.
"These heifers are just toppin' man!
Just toppin, look and see,
These udders are near perfect man,
I'm gaun tae bid for two or three".
(Now that's not a strictly accurate quote,
I have here in my hand
For Acky used some adjectives
The ladies wouldnae understand!)
But the buyers all agreed wi' him
For the biddin' went sky high,
And a record price was paid
For the ladies o' Ardross WRI!

Now a farmer needs a dog or two
To keep the beasts in line,
And wan auld bitch made such a price
I wish it had been mine!
It had wiry hair,
A glint in its eye,
And it made a hefty sum,
And it's face bore some resemblance
To the postmistress, Mrs Thom!

When the judges gave their verdict
For Supreme Champion o' the Show
They got unanimous approval
Fae the wans that's in the know.
For the Champion had a long straight back,
Broad shoulders, classic head,
Short, sturdy legs weel-fitted
For the hill life he had led.
It was generally agreed, that if a herd
Ye thocht o' startin',
The Champion was the perfect sire,
It was... auld Richie Martin!

It was just then that I woke up,
In a panic-stricken sweat,
For I'd bought the whole damned lot
And found I'd ended up in debt!

ACKNOWLEDGEMENTS:

Grateful thanks go to:
Waterstone's

•

Johnny Foxes

&

Emerald Inns

Bank Street, Inverness
Saltburn Road, Invergordon